GOD'S COMMANDS FOR LITTLES

Learning about God's laws
through poetry and rhymes

GOD'S COMMANDS FOR LITTLES

Honoring Mom & Dad

A.M LEE

To my littles, the four E's.
You are precious in mine and His sight.

We can fill our homes with love, with a little help from you,

We'll honor our parents, and they'll honor us too.

Their guidance and care, like a guiding light,

Leads us through darkness, making everything right.

In honoring parents, we do things Gods way,

Following their footsteps, day by day.

Their love and guidance, a treasure so dear,

In our hearts, forever near.

So let's honor our parents, with respect and love,

Guided by teachings from heaven above.

In their embrace, we find our home,

Honoring them, wherever we roam.

Exodus 20:12

"Honor your father and your mother, that your days may be long upon the land which the LORD your God is giving you.

3

When parents ask for help, lend a hand with glee,

For kindness and obedience make our homes happy.

Follow the rules, both big and small,

For respecting parents, God calls all.

When chores need doing,

let's jump right in, Helping them with a cheerful grin.

For in serving others, joy we find,

Bringing happiness of a special kind.

With gentle hearts, let's obey their voice,

In every moment, make the right choice.

For in respecting parents, we honor God's call,

Guiding us to love and cherish all.

Hebrews 13:16

"And do not forget to do good and to share with others, for with such sacrifices God is pleased."

With gentle hearts and voices mild,

We listen to them to tame our inner wild.

When parents speak, let's heed their call,

Doing what they say brings smiles for all.

Listening closely to what they say,

Let us follow instructions, for ears that hear are less likely to stray.

In Gods teachings, clear and true,

We learn to listen, me and you.

Colossians 3:20

Children, obey your parents in all things,
for this is well pleasing to the Lord.

When we make a mistake, let's say "I'm sorry",

It's the first step to making things feel less stormy.

For in saying sorry, we show we care,

And let love and kindness fill the air.

When parents make mistakes, let's forgive and forget,

It's a lesson in love we'll never regret.

For in forgiving, we release the pain,

And allow peace and joy in our hearts to reign.

Let us practice apologizing and forgiving each day,

Making our hearts much lighter, along the way.

For in saying sorry and letting go,

Love and happiness will surely grow and flow.

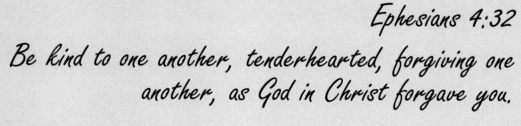

Ephesians 4:32

Be kind to one another, tenderhearted, forgiving one another, as God in Christ forgave you.

When playing with mom and dad, laughter fills the air,

With parents by your side, you won't deny they truly care.

Reading bedtime stories, cuddled up tight,

In their loving embrace, everything feels just right.

Going for walks, hand in hand,

Exploring Gods creation together, a magnificent land.

Sharing joyful moments, one by one,

Honoring our parents with quality time is tons of fun.

So let's cherish these times, big and small,

With the ones who love us, most of all.

For in sharing laughs, our bond will grow,

With every hug and every hello.

Psalm 16:11

You make known to me the path of life; in your presence there
is fullness of joy; at your right hand are pleasures forevermore.

By listening to their stories, old and new,

From parents' lips, tips for life come through.

Ask questions, big and small, curious and bright,

Learning from their knowledge, surely brings God's delight.

By observing their loving ways, day by day,

we can learn how to serve others, even learn how to pray.

Learning from their guidance, gentle and wise,

Holding their teachings, a precious prize.

So let's honor their wisdom, big and small,

In every moment, obeying Gods call.

For in learning from parents, we find our way,

Guided by their love, come what may.

Proverbs 6:20-22

My child, keep your father's commands and do not forsake your mother's teaching. Bind them upon your heart forever; fasten them around your neck. When you walk, they will guide you; when you sleep, they will watch over you; when you awake, they will speak to you.

In the quiet of the night, before we sleep,

Let's pray for our parents, in silence deep.

For God's blessings to surround them with grace,

And keep them safe in every place.

Pray for wisdom to guide them each day,

In every decision, every step of the way.

Pray for their hearts to be filled with love so bright,

So they can lead us through day and night.

Let's fold our hands and close our eyes tight,

And lift up our parents in prayers each night.

For in praying for them, God's love will bloom,

Honoring them, in every room.

Matthew 21:22

And whatever you ask in prayer, you will receive,
if you have faith.

When parents are busy or feeling tired,

Let's be patient and kind, as Gods love requires.

For in showing compassion, gentle and true,

We honor Gods teachings, old and new.

With gentle hands and voices so mild,

Let's wait with patience, with a generous smile.

For in moments of waiting, we practice love Gods way,

Bringing peace and joy and more chances to play.

So let's be kind and patient, considering others,

Honoring fathers, honoring mothers.

For in loving our parents, with hearts open wide,

We follow the teachings, with Gods love as our guide.

1 Corinthians 13:4

Love is patient and kind; love does not envy
or boast; it is not arrogant.

Remember each morning something important has to be done,

Before you can start your day of fun.

So wherever you are, even if quite far away,

Let us honor our parents before heading out to play.

Ephesians 6:1-3

Children, obey your parents in the Lord, for this is right.
Honor your father and mother, that it may go well with you
and that you may live long in the land.

18

Toddle off with a grin so wide,

To find your father, your admiration and pride.

Give a big hug to your papa so dear, and say

"Thank you, papa, for always being near"

1 Thessalonians 2:11-12

Fathers encourage and comfort their children

With a giggle and a bounce, make your way,

To where your mama works hard, day by day.

Then hug your mama tight, oh so tight,

and say "Thank you mama, for making everything right."

So let's remember, come what may,

To honor our parents every day.

As for mama's and papa's, so kind and true,

May God bless them and bless you too.

Isaiah 66:13

As a mother comforts her child, so I will comfort you.

Made in the USA
Las Vegas, NV
04 January 2025